by Iain Gray

Lang**Syne**

PUBLISHING

WRITING *to* REMEMBER

LangSyne
PUBLISHING
WRITING *to* REMEMBER

Vineyard Business Centre,
Pathhead, Midlothian EH37 5XP
Tel: 01875 321 203 Fax: 01875 321 233
E-mail: info@lang-syne.co.uk
www.langsyneshop.co.uk

Design by Dorothy Meikle
Printed by Ricoh Print Scotland
© Lang Syne Publishers Ltd 2009

ISBN 978-1-85217-267-1

McGrath

MOTTO:
Salvation by faith.

CREST:
A hand holding a Maltese Cross.

NAME variations include:
Mac Craith *(Gaelic)*
Grath
MacGra
MacGrath
MacGraw
McGraw
Magrath
Magraw

Chapter one:

Origins of Irish surnames

**According to an old saying, there are two types of Irish –
those who actually are Irish and those who wish they were.**

This sentiment is only one example of the allure that the
high romance and drama of the proud nation's history holds
for thousands of people scattered across the world today.

It's a sad fact, however, that the vast majority of Irish
surnames are found far beyond Irish shores, rather than on
the Emerald Isle itself.

The population stood at around eight million souls in
1841, but today it stands at fewer than six million.

This is mainly a tragic consequence of the potato
famine, also known as the Great Hunger, which devastated
Ireland between 1845 and 1849.

The Irish peasantry had become almost wholly reliant
for basic sustenance on the potato, first introduced from the
Americas in the seventeenth century.

When the crop was hit by a blight, at least 800,000
people starved to death while an estimated two million
others were forced to seek a new life far from their native
shores – particularly in America, Canada, and Australia.

The effects of the potato blight continued until about
1851, by which time a firm pattern of emigration had
become established.

Ireland's loss, however, was to the gain of the countries in which the immigrants settled, contributing enormously, as their descendants do today, to the well being of the nations in which their forefathers settled.

But those who were forced through dire circumstance to establish a new life in foreign parts never forgot their roots, or the proud heritage and traditions of the land that gave them birth.

Nor do their descendants.

It is a heritage that is inextricably bound up in the colourful variety of Irish names themselves – and the origin and history of these names forms an integral part of the vibrant drama that is the nation's history, one of both glorious fortune and tragic misfortune.

This history is well documented, and one of the most important and fascinating of the earliest sources are *The Annals of the Four Masters*, compiled between 1632 and 1636 by four friars at the Franciscan Monastery in County Donegal.

Compiled from earlier sources, and purporting to go back to the Biblical Deluge, much of the material takes in the mythological origins and history of Ireland and the Irish

This includes tales of successive waves of invaders and settlers such as the Fomorians, the Partholonians, the Nemedians, the Fir Bolgs, the Tuatha De Danann, and the Laigain.

Of particular interest are the *Milesian Genealogies*

because the majority of Irish clans today claim a descent from either Heremon, Ir, or Heber – three of the sons of Milesius, a king of what is now modern day Spain.

These sons invaded Ireland in the second millennium B.C, apparently in fulfilment of a mysterious prophecy received by their father.

This Milesian lineage is said to have ruled Ireland for nearly 3,000 years, until the island came under the sway of England's King Henry II in 1171 following what is known as the Cambro-Norman invasion.

This is an important date not only in Irish history in general, but for the effect the invasion subsequently had for Irish surnames.

'Cambro' comes from the Welsh, and 'Cambro-Norman' describes those Welsh knights of Norman origin who invaded Ireland.

But they were invaders who stayed, inter-marrying with the native Irish population and founding their own proud dynasties that bore Cambro-Norman names such as Archer, Barbour, Brannagh, Fitzgerald, Fitzgibbon, Fleming, Joyce, Plunkett, and Walsh – to name only a few.

These 'Cambro-Norman' surnames that still flourish throughout the world today form one of the three main categories in which Irish names can be placed – those of Gaelic-Irish, Cambro-Norman, and Anglo-Irish.

Previous to the Cambro-Norman invasion of the twelfth century, and throughout the earlier invasions and settlement of those wild bands of sea rovers known as the Vikings in the eighth and ninth centuries, the population of the island was relatively small, and it was normal for a person to be identified through the use of only a forename.

But as population gradually increased and there were many more people with the same forename, surnames were adopted to distinguish one person, or one community, from another.

Individuals identified themselves with their own particular tribe, or 'tuath', and this tribe – that also became known as a clann, or clan – took its name from some distinguished ancestor who had founded the clan.

The Gaelic-Irish form of the name Kelly, for example, is Ó Ceallaigh, or O'Kelly, indicating descent from an original 'Ceallaigh', with the 'O' denoting 'grandson of.' The name was later anglicised to Kelly.

The prefix 'Mac' or 'Mc', meanwhile, as with the clans of the Scottish Highlands, denotes 'son of.'

Although the Irish clans had much in common with their Scottish counterparts, one important difference lies in what are known as 'septs', or branches, of the clan.

Septs of Scottish clans were groups who often bore an entirely different name from the clan name but were under the clan's protection.

In Ireland, septs were groups that shared the same name and who could be found scattered throughout the four provinces of Ulster, Leinster, Munster, and Connacht.

The 'golden age' of the Gaelic-Irish clans, infused as their veins were with the blood of Celts, pre-dates the Viking invasions of the eighth and ninth centuries and the Norman invasion of the twelfth century, and the sacred heart of the country was the Hill of Tara, near the River Boyne, in County Meath.

Known in Gaelic as 'Teamhar na Rí', or Hill of Kings, it was the royal seat of the 'Ard Rí Éireann', or High King of Ireland, to whom the petty kings, or chieftains, from the island's provinces were ultimately subordinate.

It was on the Hill of Tara, beside a stone pillar known as the Irish 'Lia Fáil', or Stone of Destiny, that the High Kings were inaugurated and, according to legend, this stone would emit a piercing screech that could be heard all over Ireland when touched by the hand of the rightful king.

The Hill of Tara is today one of the island's main tourist attractions.

Opposition to English rule over Ireland, established in the wake of the Cambro-Norman invasion, broke out frequently and the harsh solution adopted by the powerful forces of the Crown was to forcibly evict the native Irish from their lands.

These lands were then granted to Protestant colonists, or 'planters', from Britain.

Many of these colonists, ironically, came from Scotland and were the descendants of the original 'Scotti', or 'Scots', who gave their name to Scotland after migrating there in the fifth century A.D., from the north of Ireland.

Colonisation entailed harsh penal laws being imposed on the majority of the native Irish population, stripping them practically of all of their rights.

The Crown's main bastion in Ireland was Dublin and its environs, known as the Pale, and it was the dispossessed peasantry who lived outside this Pale, desperately striving to eke out a meagre living.

It was this that gave rise to the modern-day expression of someone or something being 'beyond the pale'.

Attempts were made to stamp out all aspects of the ancient Gaelic-Irish culture, to the extent that even to bear a Gaelic-Irish name was to invite discrimination.

This is why many Gaelic-Irish names were anglicised with, for example, and noted above, Ó Ceallaigh, or O'Kelly, being anglicised to Kelly.

Succeeding centuries have seen strong revivals of Gaelic-Irish consciousness, however, and this has led to many families reverting back to the original form of their name, while the language itself is frequently found on the fluent tongues of an estimated 90,000 to 145,000 of the island's population.

Ireland's turbulent history of religious and political strife is one that lasted well into the twentieth century, a landmark century that saw the partition of the island into the twenty-six counties of the independent Republic of

Ireland, or Eire, and the six counties of Northern Ireland, or Ulster.

Dublin, originally founded by Vikings, is now a vibrant and truly cosmopolitan city while the proud city of Belfast is one of the jewels in the crown of Ulster.

It was Saint Patrick who first brought the light of Christianity to Ireland in the fifth century A.D.

Interpretations of this Christian message have varied over the centuries, often leading to bitter sectarian conflict – but the many intricately sculpted Celtic Crosses found all over the island are symbolic of a unity that crosses the sectarian divide.

It is an image that fuses the 'old gods' of the Celts with Christianity.

All the signs from the early years of this new millennium indicate that sectarian strife may soon become a thing of the past – with the Irish and their many kinsfolk across the world, be they Protestant or Catholic, finding common purpose in the rich tapestry of their shared heritage.

Chapter two:

The sword and the pen

Distinct groups of bearers of the proud name of McGrath were to be found from earliest times at different locations throughout the Emerald Isle.

One branch was settled in the area of the present day counties of Donegal and Fermanagh with another in the present day counties of Clare and Limerick.

Another sept, descended from the Clare and Limerick McGraths, settled near Dungarvan, in Co. Waterford – and it is here that the ruins of the twelfth century McGrath's Castle can be seen to this day.

Another branch of the McGraths also flourished for centuries in the area of present day Co. Down, having adopted the 'MacGraw' form of the name.

'McGrath', or 'MacGrath', stems from the Gaelic Mac Craith, indicating 'sons of Raith', with 'Raith' indicating 'grace', or 'prosperity'.

It is through this name that the McGraths of today can lay claim to a truly illustrious pedigree, one that stretches back through the dim mists of time to the great Irish warrior king Brian Boru, because it was the descendants of his brother, Ahearne, who eventually took the 'Mac Craith' name.

Along with other clans such as the O'Hickeys, O'Hallorans, Kennedys, McNamaras, Clanceys, O'Gormans, and O'Gradys, the McGraths were part of the mighty confederation of clans known as 'the tribe of Cas', or Dalcassians.

The kingdom of Thomond was the territory of the Dalcassians and what later became the famed O'Brien clan, and it was Boru and his Dalcassian knights, who included a McGrath, who fought in one of the most decisive battles ever to have taken place on Irish soil.

This was the battle of Clontarf, fought about four miles north of Dublin on Good Friday of 1014.

Late tenth and early eleventh century Ireland was the scene of vicious inter-clan rivalry as successive clan chiefs fought for supremacy over their rivals.

It was this disunity that worked to the advantage of the Norman invaders of the late twelfth century and the Viking invaders of previous centuries.

The period 795 A.D. to 1014 A.D. is known to Irish history as The Viking Tyranny, and it was largely through the inspired leadership of Brian Boru that Viking power was diminished.

He was able to achieve this by managing to rally a number of other chieftains to his cause – although by no means all.

With his battle-hardened Dalcassian knights at his side, Boru had by 1002A.D. achieved the prize of the High Kingship of Ireland – but there were still rival chieftains, and not least the Vikings, to deal with.

These Vikings, known as Ostmen, had occupied and

fortified Dublin in the mid-ninth century and had other important trading settlements on other parts of the island.

Resenting Boru's High Kingship, a number of chieftains, particularly those of the province of Leinster, found common cause with the Ostmen, and the two sides met in final and bloody confrontation at Clontarf.

Boru proved victorious, but the annals speak of great slaughter on the day, with the dead piled high on the field of battle, including three of his sons.

The warrior king had little time to celebrate his victory – being killed in his tent by a party of fleeing Vikings, but not before felling most of them with his great two-handed sword.

Before his death Brian Boru had organised the Dalcassian clans in such a manner that they all had their own functions within the confederation as a whole.

It was the important distinction of the McGraths to act as hereditary bards – recording in poetry stirring and poignant tales of glorious deeds, battles won, and battles lost.

This is a McGrath tradition that has continued for centuries: John Mac Craith was the author in the late fourteenth century of *The Wars of Turlough*, while Andrew McGrath was a noted late eighteenth century Irish poet.

The McGrath bards would also have recorded what is undoubtedly one of the most significant events in Irish history – the late twelfth century Norman invasion of the island and the subsequent domination of the forces of the English Crown.

Twelfth century Ireland was far from being a unified nation, split up as it was into territories ruled over by squabbling chieftains who ruled as kings in their own right – and this inter-clan rivalry worked to the advantage of the invaders.

In a series of bloody conflicts one chieftain, or king, would occasionally gain the upper hand over his rivals, and by 1156 the most powerful was Muirchertach MacLochlainn, king of the O'Neills.

Rory O'Connor, king of the province of Connacht, opposed him but he increased his power and influence by allying himself with Dermot MacMurrough, king of Leinster.

MacLochlainn and MacMurrough were aware that the main key to the kingdom of Ireland was the thriving trading port of Dublin that had been established by invading Vikings in 852 A.D.

Dublin was taken by the combined forces of the Leinster and Connacht kings, but when MacLochlainn died the Dubliners rose up in revolt and overthrew the unpopular MacMurrough.

A triumphant Rory O'Connor entered Dublin and was later inaugurated as Ard Rí, or High King, but MacMurrough refused to accept defeat.

He appealed for help from England's Henry II in unseating O'Connor, an act that was to radically affect the future course of Ireland's fortunes.

The English monarch agreed to help MacMurrough, but

distanced himself from direct action by delegating his Norman subjects in Wales with the task.

These ambitious and battle-hardened barons and knights had first settled in Wales following the Norman Conquest of England in 1066 and, with an eye on rich booty, plunder, and lands, were only too eager to obey their sovereign's wishes and furnish MacMurrough with aid.

MacMurrough rallied powerful barons such as Robert Fitzstephen and Maurice Fitzgerald to his cause, along with Gilbert de Clare, Earl of Pembroke.

The mighty Norman war machine soon moved into action, and so fierce and disciplined was their onslaught on the forces of Rory O'Connor and his allies that by 1171 they had re-captured Dublin, in the name of MacMurrough, and other strategically important territories.

Henry II now began to take cold feet over the venture, realising that he may have created a rival in the form of a separate Norman kingdom in Ireland. Accordingly, he landed on the island, near Waterford, at the head of a large army in October of 1171 with the aim of curbing the power of his Cambro-Norman barons. But protracted war between the king and his barons was averted when they submitted to the royal will, promising homage and allegiance in return for holding the territories they had conquered in the king's name.

Henry also received the reluctant submission and homage of many of the Irish chieftains, and English dominion over Ireland was ratified through the Treaty of

Windsor of 1175, under the terms of which Rory O'Connor, for example, was allowed to rule territory unoccupied by the Normans in the role of a vassal of the king.

It was a recipe for disaster, further exacerbated as increasing waves of English adventurers descended on the island – at the expense of native Irish clans such as the McGraths.

An indication of the harsh treatment meted out to them can be found in a desperate plea sent to Pope John XII by Roderick O'Carroll of Ely, Donald O'Neil of Ulster, and a number of other Irish chieftains in 1318.

They stated: 'As it very constantly happens, whenever an Englishman, by perfidy or craft, kills an Irishman, however noble, or however innocent, be he clergy or layman, there is no penalty or correction enforced against the person who may be guilty of such wicked murder.

'But rather the more eminent the person killed and the higher rank which he holds among his own people, so much more is the murderer honoured and rewarded by the English, and not merely by the people at large, but also by the religious and bishops of the English race.'

This appeal to the Pope had little effect on what became an increasingly brutal policy of the occupying English Crown against the native Irish such as the McGraths.

But resistance did not only take the form of written appeals, as the island was swept over succeeding centuries by a series of bloody rebellions in which the McGraths played no small part.

Chapter three:
Flames of rebellion

Incitement to rebellion came in what was the detested form of the English Crown's policy of 'plantation', or settlement of loyal Protestants on land held by native Irish such as the McGraths.

This started during the reign from 1491 to 1547 of Henry VIII, whose Reformation effectively outlawed the established Roman Catholic faith throughout his dominions, and continued throughout the subsequent reigns of Elizabeth I, James I (James VI of Scotland), and in the wake of the devastating Cromwellian invasion of 1649.

In what is known as the Nine Years War, a number of Irish earls had rebelled against the policy of plantation and harsh penal policies against Catholics.

Following their defeat at the battle of Kinsale in 1601 and the final suppression of the rebellion three years later in Ulster, their future existence hung by a precarious thread.

Three years later, in September of 1607 and in what is known as The Flight of the Earls, Hugh O'Neill, 2nd Earl of Tyrone and Rory O'Donnell, 1st Earl of Tyrconnel, sailed into foreign exile from the village of Rathmullan, on the shore of Lough Swilly, in Co. Donegal, accompanied by ninety loyal followers.

The event is recognised today as having signalled the final collapse of the ancient Gaelic order.

The failed rebellion only served to further consolidate the Crown's tenacious grip on Ireland and further the policy of plantation, particularly in the northern province of Ulster.

In an insurrection that exploded in 1641, at least 2,000 Protestant settlers were massacred at the hands of Catholic landowners and their native Irish peasantry, while thousands more were stripped of their belongings and driven from their lands to seek refuge where they could.

Terrible as the atrocities were against the Protestant settlers, subsequent accounts became greatly exaggerated, serving to fuel a burning desire for revenge against the rebels.

Tragically for Ireland, this revenge became directed not only against the rebels, but native Irish Catholics such as the McGraths in general.

The English Civil War intervened to prevent immediate action against the rebels, but following the execution of Charles I in 1649 and the consolidation of the power of England's fanatically Protestant Oliver Cromwell, the time was ripe for revenge.

The Lord Protector, as he was named, descended on Ireland at the head of a 20,000-strong army that landed at Ringford, near Dublin, in August of 1649, and the consequences of this Cromwellian conquest still resonate throughout the island today.

Cromwell had three main aims: to quash all forms of

rebellion, to 'remove' all Catholic landowners who had taken part in the rebellion, and to convert the native Irish to the Protestant faith. An early warning of the terrors that were in store for the native Catholic Irish came when the northeastern town of Drogheda was stormed and taken in September and between 2,000 and 4,000 of its inhabitants killed, including priests who were summarily put to the sword. The defenders of Drogheda's St. Peter's Church, who had refused to surrender, were burned to death as they huddled for refuge in the steeple and the church was deliberately torched.

A similar fate awaited Wexford, on the southeast coast, when at least 1,500 of its inhabitants were slaughtered, including 200 defenceless women, despite their pathetic pleas for mercy.

Cromwell soon held the land in a grip of iron, allowing him to implement what amounted to a policy of ethnic cleansing.

His troopers were given free rein to hunt down and kill priests, and these included the Franciscan friar Myles McGrath, murdered in 1650.

An estimated eleven million acres of land were confiscated, while an edict was issued stating that any native Irish found east of the River Shannon after May 1, 1654 faced either summary execution or transportation to the West Indies.

A further blow against the ancient Gaelic way of life of clans such as the McGraths came through what is known in Ireland as Cogadh an Dá Rí, or The War of the Two Kings

Also known as the Williamite War in Ireland or the Jacobite War in Ireland, it was sparked off in 1688 when the Stuart monarch James II (James VII of Scotland) was deposed and fled into exile in France.

The Protestant William of Orange and his wife Mary (ironically a daughter of James II) were invited to take up the thrones of Scotland, Ireland, and England – but James still had significant support in Ireland, with his supporters known as Jacobites.

Following the arrival in England of William and Mary from Holland, Richard Talbot, 1st Earl of Tyrconnell and James's Lord Deputy in Ireland, assembled an army loyal to the Stuart cause.

The aim was to garrison and fortify the island in the name of James and quell any resistance.

Londonderry, or Derry, proved loyal to the cause of William of Orange, or William III as he had become, and managed to hold out against a siege that was not lifted until July 28, 1689.

James, with the support of troops and money supplied by Louis XIV of France, had landed at Kinsale in March of 1689 and joined forces with his Irish supporters.

A series of military encounters followed, culminating in James's defeat by an army commanded by William at the battle of the Boyne on July 12, 1689.

James fled again into French exile, never to return, while another significant Jacobite defeat occurred in July of 1691 at the battle of Aughrim – with about half their army killed on the field, wounded, or taken prisoner.

The Williamite forces besieged Limerick and the Jacobites were forced into surrender in September of 1691.

A peace treaty, known as the Treaty of Limerick followed, under which those Jacobites willing to swear an oath of loyalty to William were allowed to remain in their native land.

Those reluctant to do so, including many native Irish such as the McGraths, were allowed to seek exile on foreign shores – but their ancient homelands were lost to them forever.

A further flight overseas occurred following an abortive rebellion in 1798.

The roots of the 1798 Rising are tangled in the thick undergrowth of Irish history, but in essence it was sparked of by a fusion of sectarian and agrarian unrest and a burning desire for political reform that had been shaped by the French revolutionary slogan of 'liberty, equality, and fraternity.'

A movement had come into existence that embraced middle-class intellectuals and the oppressed peasantry, and if this loosely bound movement could be said to have had a leader, it was Wolfe Tone, a Protestant from Kildare and leading light of a radical republican movement known as the United Irishmen.

Despite attempts by the British government to concede a degree of agrarian and political reform, it was a case of far too little and much too late, and by 1795 the United

Irishmen, through Wolfe Tone, were receiving help from France – Britain's enemy.

A French invasion fleet was despatched to Ireland in December of 1796, but it was scattered by storms off Bantry Bay.

Two years later, in the summer of 1798, rebellion broke out on the island.

The first flames of revolt were fanned in Ulster, but soon died out, only to be replaced by a much more serious conflagration centred mainly in Co. Wexford.

Rebel victory was achieved at the battle of Oulart Hill, followed by another victory at the battle of Three Rocks, but the mainly peasant army was no match for the 20,000 troops or so that descended on Wexford.

Defeat followed at the battle of Vinegar Hill on 21 June, followed by another decisive defeat at Kilcumney Hill five days later.

The Rising of 1798 at last came to an exhausted conclusion, with all hope of republican victory quashed – it would not be until the early years of the twentieth century that it would at last be achieved.

Among the rebels of 1798 was a John Magrath. He was captured but managed to escape and seek refuge in America.

His son, Andrew Condon Magrath, born in 1813, became a prominent judge, a governor of Carolina, and a leading Confederate during the American Civil War.

He died in 1893.

Chapter four:

On the world stage

Bearers of the McGrath name have achieved celebrity in a colourful range of pursuits, not least in the world of film.

Born in 1951 in Timmins, Ontario, **Derek McGrath** is the Canadian actor best known to international audiences for his role as Andy Schroeder in the American sitcom *Cheers*.

The actor, who has also had roles in *Star Trek: Voyager* and *Doc*, also appears in the Canadian sitcom *Little Mosque on the Prairie*.

Best known for his role as Wooster in the television series *Wagon Train*, **Frank McGrath** was the American actor born in 1903 in Mound City, Missouri, and who died in 1967.

Born in Sydney in 1942, **Judith McGrath** is the Australian actress who played the role of deputy governor Colleen Powell in the highly popular television series *Prisoner: Cell Block H*, while behind the camera lens **Joseph McGrath**, born in 1930 in Glasgow, is the Scottish film director and screenwriter also known as Joe 'Apocalypse' McGrath or Croisette Meubles.

Memorable films he has been involved in include the 1967 *Casino Royale* and the 1969 *The Magic Christian*.

Also on the stage **John McGrath**, born in 1935 in Liverpool of Irish stock and who died in 2002, was the acclaimed playwright and supporter of the cause of Scottish independence best remembered for his work with the 7:84 Theatre Company and the play *The Cheviot, The Stag, and the Black Black Oil*.

Born in 1956 **Rory McGrath** is the English comic actor whose British television appearances include as a panel member on the popular BBC sports quiz *They Think It's All Over*, while in the world of the printed word **Harold MacGrath**, who also used the spelling 'McGrath', was a best-selling American novelist and screenwriter.

Born in 1871 in Syracuse, New York, he moved from reporter and columnist with the Syracuse Herald newspaper to author of a range of novels that included the genres of mystery and spies to romance and adventure.

His first novel, the 1899 *Arms and the Woman*, became a best-seller – setting the trend for further productions from his gifted pen, with no less than eighteen of his forty novels and three of his short stories adapted for the screen and three books adapted for the Broadway stage.

It was thanks to MacGrath that a young actor took what would become his famous screen name of Boris Karloff.

The actor took the name from the character of a mad Russian scientist in the 1920 MacGrath novel *The Drums of Jeopardy*.

McGrath died in 1932.

In contemporary times **Patrick McGrath**, born in 1950 in London, is the British novelist and master of the gothic genre whose books include the 1989 *Grotesque*, filmed as *The Grotesque* in 1995, while his novels *Spider* and *Asylum* have also been filmed.

In the world of music Christopher McGrath, born in 1978 in Berwyn, Illinois, is better known as **Gunner McGrath** – a great grandson of the English science fiction writer H.G. Wells and the lead singer and guitarist with the punk rock band Much the Same.

Born in 1968 in Hartford, Connecticut, **Mark McGrath** is the lead singer of American rock band Sugar Ray and who also makes regular television appearances including as a judge on *American Idol*.

In the world of architecture **Raymond McGrath**, born in 1903 in Sydney and who died in 1977, was a noted Australian architect and interior designer.

McGraths who have stamped their mark on ecclesiastical affairs include **Father Desmond McGrath**, the Canadian priest and trade union organiser in Newfoundland and Labrador who was responsible for the founding of the Fish, Food and Allied Workers Union.

Born in Dublin in 1945 and ordained to the priesthood in 1970, Patrick Joseph McGrath, better known as **P.J McGrath** is, at the time of writing, the second Roman Catholic Bishop of San Jose, California, a position he has held since 1999.

One of the world's leading Christian theologians is **Alister E. McGrath**, born in 1953 in Belfast.

With university degrees in both molecular biophysics and theology, he is a vigorous opponent of atheism and his books include the 2004 *The Twilight of Atheism* and the 2007 *The Dawkins Delusion?*

At the time of writing he is professor of historical theology at Oxford University.

In the highly competitive world of sport **Jeremy McGrath**, born in 1971 in San Francisco, is the Supercross motorcycle racer known as 'The King' or 'Showtime', and reckoned to be the greatest Supercross rider of all time.

At the time of writing he has won seventy-two 250cc Main Event races, while taking seven 250cc Championships wins.

Also in the world of dangerous high speed **Jack McGrath**, born in Los Angles in 1919, was the American racecar driver who was the first winner, in 1946, of the California Roadster Association Championship.

Known as 'King of the Hot Rods', he was killed in a race in Phoenix, Arizona, in 1955.

On the cricket field **Glenn McGrath**, nicknamed 'Pigeon', is the former Australian cricketer who was born in 1970 in Dubbo, New South Wales.

Regarded as one of the most outstanding fast-medium pace bowlers in cricketing history, his last games were during the 2007 Cricket World Cup.

In the world of European football **Paul McGrath**, born in 1959 in London to a Nigerian father and an Irish mother, is the former defender who played for the Republic of Ireland team from 1985 to 1997 and whose former clubs include Manchester United, Aston Villa, and Sheffield United.

Born in Manchester in 1938 **John McGrath** was the talented football defender and latterly manager who began his career with Bury in 1956 and later went on to play with teams that included Newcastle United and Southampton.

He died in 1998.

In contemporary times **John McGrath**, born in 1980 in Limerick, is the Irish midfielder who, at the time of writing, plays for English team Burton Albion.

McGraths have also been prominent in the world of politics.

Born in 1903 in Woonsocket, Rhode Island, **J. Howard McGrath** was the American Democratic party politician whose many high level positions included those of U.S. Senator, chairman of the Democratic National Committee and, from 1949 to 1952, Attorney General of the United States.

He died in 1966.

Over the border with Canada **James McGrath**, born in 1932, is the former Progressive Conservative party politician who served as Lieutenant-Governor of Newfoundland and Labrador from 1986 until 1991.

John J. McGrath, born in 1872 in Limerick, became the Democratic U.S Representative for California from 1933 to 1939 after immigrating to America from his native Ireland.

Born in Dublin in 1887 **Joseph McGrath** was the Irish politician and republican who fought in the abortive Easter Rising of 1916.

Known in Irish as Éiri Amach na Cásca, the Rising followed the posting of a proclamation of independence.

Mounted by the combined forces of the Irish Citizen Army (I.C.A.) and the Irish Republican Brotherhood (I.R.B.), the aim was to wrest independence from Britain by force of arms.

Accordingly, on April 24, Easter Monday, the combined republican forces of the I.C.A. and the I.R.B. seized strategic locations throughout Dublin, including the General Post Office.

Other Risings were timed to take place simultaneously throughout the counties of Galway, Wexford, and Louth.

But with a force of less than 5,000 republicans matched against no less than 16,000 well armed and trained troops and 1,000 armed police, the Rising was doomed to failure.

It came to a bloody and exhausted conclusion on April 30 after its leaders were forced into reluctant surrender.

More than 1,200 republicans, troops, police, and civilians had been killed, but further deaths followed as the sixteen leaders of the Rising were executed by the British Crown in Dublin's Kilmainham Jail.

Joseph McGrath was imprisoned for a time in England for his part in the Rising, but later served as a Sinn Féin member in the first Irish Dáil, or Parliament.

Turning to the world of business following his resignation from politics in 1924, he later founded the Irish Hospitals' Trust and its associated sweepstakes.

He also became Ireland's most prominent racehorse owner and breeder, before his death in 1966, winning the Epsom Derby in 1951 with Arctic Prince.

McGraths have also achieved an enduring legacy by stamping their names on the landscape – in the form of cities of the name in Alaska and in Aitken County, Minnesota.

Key dates in Ireland's history from the first settlers to the formation of the Irish Republic:

circa 7000 B.C.	Arrival and settlement of Stone Age people.
circa 3000 B.C.	Arrival of settlers of New Stone Age period.
circa 600 B.C.	First arrival of the Celts.
200 A.D.	Establishment of Hill of Tara, Co. Meath, as seat of the High Kings.
circa 432 A.D.	Christian mission of St. Patrick.
800-920 A.D.	Invasion and subsequent settlement of Vikings.
1002 A.D.	Brian Boru recognised as High King.
1014	Brian Boru killed at battle of Clontarf.
1169-1170	Cambro-Norman invasion of the island.
1171	Henry II claims Ireland for the English Crown.
1366	Statutes of Kilkenny ban marriage between native Irish and English.
1529-1536	England's Henry VIII embarks on religious Reformation.
1536	Earl of Kildare rebels against the Crown.
1541	Henry VIII declared King of Ireland.
1558	Accession to English throne of Elizabeth I.
1565	Battle of Affane.
1569-1573	First Desmond Rebellion.
1579-1583	Second Desmond Rebellion.
1594-1603	Nine Years War.
1606	Plantation' of Scottish and English settlers.
1607	Flight of the Earls.
1632-1636	Annals of the Four Masters compiled.
1641	Rebellion over policy of plantation and other grievances.
1649	Beginning of Cromwellian conquest.
1688	Flight into exile in France of Catholic Stuart monarch James II as Protestant Prince William of Orange invited to take throne of England along with his wife, Mary.
1689	William and Mary enthroned as joint monarchs; siege of Derry.
1690	Jacobite forces of James defeated by William at battle of the Boyne (July) and Dublin taken.

1691	Athlone taken by William; Jacobite defeats follow at Aughrim, Galway, and Limerick; conflict ends with Treaty of Limerick (October) and Irish officers allowed to leave for France.
1695	Penal laws introduced to restrict rights of Catholics; banishment of Catholic clergy.
1704	Laws introduced constricting rights of Catholics in landholding and public office.
1728	Franchise removed from Catholics.
1791	Foundation of United Irishmen republican movement.
1796	French invasion force lands in Bantry Bay.
1798	Defeat of Rising in Wexford and death of United Irishmen leaders Wolfe Tone and Lord Edward Fitzgerald.
1800	Act of Union between England and Ireland.
1803	Dublin Rising under Robert Emmet.
1829	Catholics allowed to sit in Parliament.
1845-1849	The Great Hunger: thousands starve to death as potato crop fails and thousands more emigrate.
1856	Phoenix Society founded.
1858	Irish Republican Brotherhood established.
1873	Foundation of Home Rule League.
1893	Foundation of Gaelic League.
1904	Foundation of Irish Reform Association.
1913	Dublin strikes and lockout.
1916	Easter Rising in Dublin and proclamation of an Irish Republic.
1917	Irish Parliament formed after Sinn Fein election victory.
1919-1921	War between Irish Republican Army and British Army.
1922	Irish Free State founded, while six northern counties remain part of United Kingdom as Northern Ireland or Ulster; civil war up until 1923 between rival republican groups.
1949	Foundation of Irish Republic after all remaining constitutional links with Britain are severed.